Introduction

Dogs; described by many as man's best friends and overtime they have proven to us that they can be more than just fur, four-feet, tail-waggling canines. Dogs have become an integral part of our lives and should be treated as another member of the family. It is very important to welcome these beautiful creatures with wide open hands in order to ensure for a smooth transition into the human community.

Just as it with babies, dogs have feelings that they cannot always clearly communicate to us; their moods, feelings, state of mind and so on have to be properly noticed in order to understand how they feel. For the dog however, the most it can do is to bark or whimper and we as humans in turn try to understand how they are feeling.

Big Cats roar, growl and snarl, small ones meow, bats screech Etc.; all in a bid to express themselves with hopes that they can be understood. Dogs howl and bark in order to communicate certain emotions, feelings and so on and it is very important for humans to understand that barking or howling is not always a sign of discontentment or a way to express rage, there are several factors that influence this expression. It could be as a result of their environment, other dogs or a host of other reasons therefore it is very important to pay attention to these expressions in a bid to properly understand the reason(s) behind them and understand your dog's needs.

Overtime, a dog's bark has been seen as a provocative, disturbing sound and this has been seen as a problem in the human society. Pet owners particularly attempt to take various measures to prevent their canine friends from "making noise". Neighbors have had major disagreements because of this 'noise'; disagreements that had to be settled in courtrooms. It is very important to know that a dog's bark is simply a way for it to express itself and by paying attention to this gesture we earn its trust and obedience.

How can you understand your dog and prevent it from barking endlessly in a bid to be heard? This can be done by simply paying rapt attention to the pet in a bid to understanding the cause for its endless barking and putting an end to it. In doing this, guessing is not enough therefore it is necessary to take it up and understand your Dog. Once this is done, you will definitely enjoy a better relationship with your dog and this is in your best interest as a pet owner and also in the interest of your canine companion.

As you go on with the pages of this interesting, eye-opening manual it is very important to keep in mind that patience is a very important factor when it comes to understanding your dog and satisfying its needs. Come with me let's put an end to your pet's endless barking, would you?

Chapter 1
The Basics on Barking Dogs

"Why do dogs bark?" Almost every dog owner has had to answer this question from an inquisitive toddler who seeks knowledge. Historically, dogs are descendants of wolves although they have been domesticated and this is the reason for the obvious differences in character. Dogs have been known to howl for a bunch of reasons ranging from fear, anxiety, communicating and so on. The question still remains, 'why do they bark?' This question can be given a simple analogy to simplify the answer, 'why do humans talk'? Unlike the wolves who howl (in a somewhat scary manner), dogs bark often and for various reasons at various times.

While humans use speech as a means of communication, dogs bark to communicate. Ordinarily you would probably assume that every time your dog barks, it is making the same sound but upon closer observation you will likely realize that there are various pitches and sounds that they make to convey different messages to other beings. Rather than being bothered by your dog's bark, you should be more concerned if your dog doesn't bark, barking is the way through which they can "talk" to us and tell us how they feel or think. As wagging tails tell us that our dogs are happy, barking can tell us a thing or two about how the dog is feeling at every point in time.

According to veterinary behaviorists, the bark evolved over time as a complicated means of communication between man and his canine best friend and also as a means of communication amongst dogs. There are several reasons why dogs bark and most of them if not all are influenced by pet owners indirectly. The increased tendency of the dog to bark could have been very useful to humans in that it would have provided an early warning system. Since dogs were domesticated centuries ago, their physical appearance had been altered; various dogs bark for various reasons ranging from the need to be attended to, to the need to communicate or to express excitement or displeasure with the things around them.

Have you ever witnesses heavy rainfall; I mean those kinds of rainfall that come with thunder and lightning? Being around a dog in these kinds of moments will show you the effects that these kinds of natural catastrophes have on animals. It primarily makes them restless and eventually causes them to be really scared; they tend to feel anxious when these kinds of situations occur. The discomfort felt by these canines is not restricted to natural catastrophes; loud noise from guns, fireworks can also cause them to be defiant and uneasy.

As I said earlier, it takes patience when you are trying to understand your dog, when you hear them barking or you notice any form of unease, shouting should never be an option. There are better ways of training them or instill some sort of discipline in them, but you need to patiently correct them because they are more likely to learn from you in a positive and friendly manner rather than when you try to teach them in a rather harsh manner. Overtime I have learnt that people tend to overreact to hearing their dogs bark, you should know that there are reasons behind their barking. The best thing to do is to find out what the reasons are and then respond positively. It could be some form of threat that they feel and it will not be proper to shut them up when they are signaling for your attention because they trust you to handle whatever threat that they may feel.

Chapter 2
Dogs Make Sounds to Communicate With You

It is always frustrating for dog owners when your dog cannot seem to be quite and it keeps barking, most dog owners are cool with it when their dogs bark at other dogs or when it barks to intimate us about a particular threat. On other occasions when it seems like the dog's barking is becoming endless, it can be really frustrating to the owner of the dog and people around you. Before you abruptly conclude that it is a barking problem, take out time to understand the reason behind it. A dog has clear reasons for every kind of sound it makes, and it is important to recognize the reason behind each one. When you recognize the reasons behind it, it will be easier to reward your dog for barking whenever it barks for a benefiting purpose. By doing this, you are encouraging the dog to bark for reasons that you will eventually find to be benefiting. A dog's bark could alert you about various things like food, the need to poo, the need for a walk and so on. For this purpose, it is necessary to train your dog to do things on cue and not just for attention purpose. By teaching your dog to be quiet at most times, it learns to device other less noisy methods of getting things done.

Often times, excessive barking could be a problem with the behavior of the dog and it can be caused by a number of things. In curbing the problem, firstly it is important to understand what the cause is then you can change the things that trigger these kinds of reactions in your dog. As a pet owner, it is your duty to study and subsequently know your dog so well that you can identify what the problem is by just listening to the dog's bark. You should be able to decide if your dog wants to play or if your dog wants to eat or just play in the yard simply by listening to its bark.

Most pet owners just wish that their dog can stop barking suddenly, this cannot happen without a conscious effort to put in time into training the pet. It will take quite some time to teach your dog to stop barking (as often as it does) because it is something that should be taught by you and like most learning processes, it takes quite some time to get a hang of it.

Wishing for your dog to stop barking altogether is actually impossible (that will be like hooping for a child that cannot talk). Therefore, the goal should be to reduce the frequency of the dog's bark rather than totally eliminating the gesture, also it is very important to note that while some dogs are more likely to bark, others are not likely to; it all depends on the breed of the dog in question. As humans, we have varying levels of tolerance when it comes to our response to the barking of a dog; some of us can stand barking dogs to an extent while it gets some people really pissed off. Our level of tolerance is also highly influenced by the people around us and how they feel about the perceived 'noise' that your pet makes. Overtime I have come to the realization that there are various commands that can correct dogs and prevent them from barking excessively. It is important that you recognize these commands and then train your dog to understand them too. By doing this, the art of training your dog will be as simple as teaching it to know its name.

Chapter 3
Dispelling the Myths About Barking

Often times, humans tend to point towards the supernatural when it comes to explaining animal behavior and actions. We often take ghosts or evil spirits as the cause of a dog's howl. Often times, we are too lazy to take out time to find out what the reason behind a dog's howl is and we automatically attribute it to some unseen forces. I have patiently done some study and I have found out some cool facts about barking dogs.
These are 7 facts that I discovered;

THE DOG BARKS ON PURPOSE- Most owners of pets are quick to jump to the false conclusion that the barking of a dog is the fault of the dog. Many people tend to assume that the dog can control it but intentionally doesn't do that. According to researchers, there is always a reason behind a dog's bark and it is better to find out these reasons because that is the only way by which you can prevent the dog from barking constantly and unnecessarily because in all honesty, it is not the fault of the dog that it barks.

Most times pet owners forget to concentrate on the more important factor which is finding out why their dogs are barking. Instead of taking out time to do this, they just get angry at the innocent dog who just wants its need to be responded to by an owner who is caring enough to pay attention and discover why the dog s barking.

I ASKED MY DOG TO STOP BARKING THEREFORE IT SHOULD- Most dog owners tend to see their dogs as being rude or constituting a nuisance when it tends to bark too often. It is important to understand the fact that your dog only bark when it has certain needs; it might need to eat, take a walk because it is lonely or because of several reasons. Knowing this, you would understand that the dog is not obliged to stop barking just because you said so; you have to respond to the needs of the dog for it to stop barking endlessly.

MY NEIGHBORS ARE THE CAUSES- One of the main reasons why dog owners get pissed at their dogs for barking is because of their neighbors who probably complain about the noise of the dog. Often times, some go as far as accusing their neighbors of being the reason why the dog keeps barking, no one should have that kind of power over your dog because they are a member of your family and it is your responsibility that they are not being made uncomfortable, if you must change the location of the dog to prevent it from being teased/ harassed then you should do it.

THE BEST WATCHDOGS ARE THE ONES THAT BARK- This misconception is common among dog owners who tend to believe that the more a dog barks then the more useful it will be as a watchdog. The truth is that all dogs bark, the ones that know the right times and the right reasons for which they need to bark are the ones that are the best watchdogs and it takes adequate training for you to be able to do this.

MY DOG ONLY BARKS IN MY ABSENCE- More often than not, dogs tends to do the most barking when they are left alone. This is why it seems like you are always greeted with news of how your dog was barking all day long and disturbing the peace of people around you. It might be worth considering the fact that the dog might be experiencing loneliness, and this could cause it to bark endlessly.

BARKING IS NORMAL, GET OVER IT- All animals have one thing in common, they communicate with their likes and other creatures through gestures, sounds and so on. Considering this fact will make you realize that your dog's bark might be as a result of certain factors therefore it is important to understand the reason for your dog's barking instead of being angry by the fact that it is barking.

YES! YOUR DOG CAN BE TRAINED- Your dog can be trained to sit, listen to its name, and carry out orders amongst other things. Although some people wrongly assume that this is not possible, but I am here to take away your doubts and reassure you that you can train your dog to ensure that it stops barking.

and stimulated will be more active and would learn to bark for other important reasons. By doing this, you are going to reduce or obliterate chronic barking in your dog.

Chapter 5
4 Immediate Solutions

Different people might give various explanations for a barking dog and although we will certainly arrive at a consensus that most times, the dog's bark isn't actually threatening and there is no doubt that it could have its advantages.

Dog barking has several explanations. Yes, it's not threatening and can certainly be useful; but too loud, too often, is annoying. Left as it is, barking leads to some problems. The most common problem would come from neighbors complaining.

The internet is the home where there is practically an answer to every question asked; questions regarding problems concerning pets have increased immensely. It is also very advisable to visit a vet regularly concerning your pet. This is important because in order to solve the problem, we need to understand what the problem is and have sufficient knowledge regarding the subject natter and the various behaviors that it exhibits. Once individuals begin to notice these signs, it is important to share the ideas and solutions in order to help others and get similar help in your time of need. Some ideas I have developed, and I believe will be very helpful in the bid to stop your dog from barking endlessly. Here are some tips that will help you deal properly with the barking problem that your dog has. Exchanging ideas and sharing solutions can be most helpful! The key to controlling any problem is by understanding what could trigger the behavior and how to deal with it. This holds true to any problems and thus could be used to deal with the dog barking. Below are helpful ways to deal with your dog's barking problem:

1. REGULAR AND HEALTHY FEEDING- Dogs always bark when they are thirsty, and they have various sounds (based on their breed) that they make when they need to be fed. By feeding them regularly, you are able to condition them to eat around certain

Chapter 4
No one Likes Constant Barking

No matter how cute or lovely a dog is or may seem to be, it becomes less cute when it begins to bark excessively. The discomfort that comes with an excessively barking dog is felt by not just yourself and your canine companion; it is felt by everyone who is around you and they can attest to the frustration of having a dog that barks excessively.

Often times, dogs bark at strangers in out of a discomfort that occurs with seeing a new face on your property, this could probably pass for the loudest noise that dogs make as it may be accompanied why loud growls. In these kinds of situations, my singular advice remains that you should remove the dog from the reach of strangers or you can decide to give your dog a solemn reassurance to make it feel like everything will be alright and that you care about its safety. Summarily, you need to find out the source of discomfort and remove it to ensure that your dog lives comfortably.

Ever had those times when your dog was up in the middle of the night with a loud howl and follows it up with hours of barking? These kinds of occurrences might be frustrating and might cause us to wake up abruptly from time to time therefore causing you to sleep for less number of hours. Neighbors are the victims and they suffer this same fate with us even though they do not own the dog. This could be really frustrating and for this reason if constant complaining to you as the owner might not make so much difference, such a neighbor can decide to take matters into his own hands and hurt the dog either by means of poisoning or any other deadly means of showing their frustrations. Train your dog to stop barking unnecessarily and you might just be saving such a dog's life or preventing it from imminent danger

Apart from the harm that could be inflicted to your dog, chronic barking could be really detrimental to her physical health and should be dealt with. A bored dog is definitely more likely to bark endlessly, it is necessary to take your dogs on walks in order to exercise her and ensure that she barks less than the chronic barking dog. Exercise your dog today and you will be taking away over a 50% likelihood of chronic barking. Exercise your dog regularly to ensure that it doesn't stay bored or dull. A dog that feels active types and by doing this with healthy meals will definitely cause your dog to make less noise.

2. REGULAR EXERCISE IS A NECESSITY- Your dog has a lot of energy and energy reserves, if it doesn't shed the energy, it will likely become very jumpy. Take out your calendar and plan your walks with your dog because it is just as important as other things that you pay attention to. On days when the weather isn't in its best behavior, you can get creative with indoor activities to ensure that your dog gets a regular dose of exercise and stays healthy.

3. YOUR DOG NEEDS A COMPANION IN YOUR ABSENCE- Dogs get really anxious when they feel the signs of loneliness and solitude, get another dog or at the very least, get toys that will continually keep your dog calm. It is also important to know and respect the fact that your dog sees everything that you do and gets jealous if it seems like you are giving attention that is due to it to another dog or pet.

4. TEACH YOUR DOG WHEN TO BARK AND WHEN NOT TO- As a pet owner, it is almost impossible for your pet not to listen when you give out orders like 'come', 'sit' and so on. It is also important to be able to dictate to your dogs the kind of situations in which it is inappropriate and those in which it is appropriate to bark.

Chapter 6

Advice From Your Friends

As you might have guessed, I am a dog owner too and I once had the problem of putting my dog to control when it came to her barking. I picked up my devices and I sent a bunch of messages out to my friends in order to get advice from their experiences too. After a rigorous process of trying to pick out the advice that I got, I finally settled for a couple of them that I will love to share.

1. Get you a dog that respects and obeys you all the time. Shouting will not work because it could make the dog feel like you are barking too, and it will only complicate matters more.

2. Consistency is the key when trying to train a dog. Choose words that you will use consistently in correcting or applauding their behaviors or gestures.

3. I mentioned earlier that patience is a key ingredient when it comes to trying to instill knowledge into your pet. Be patient with the dog and also with yourself, Rome was not built in a day therefore remember that it is a process and it wouldn't happen suddenly.

4. As much as we always ensure to punish dogs in order to make them understand that certain behaviors are bad, it is also very important to reward them for good behavior because they remember rewards more than punishments. A simple pat on the chest or a commendation is an acceptable reward too.

5. Dogs fear too and they also have the ability to see and understand their environment. Therefore, it is wrong to hug your pet suddenly or too tightly that it begins to feel some sort of insecurity.

6. You can only teach your dog these steps and ensure they have mastered it by putting them through regular test which will be made to look real. By doing this you are ensuring that your dog better understands you at all times.

If you have made attempts and you are still not convinced about the barking of you dog, then it is necessary to see a veterinary doctor or an expert when it comes to understanding animal behavior.

Chapter 7

There are Reasons Why Dogs Bark

To understand something, you need to know the motive behind it as it will give you a proper insight into the subject matter. This principle also applies to owning a barking pet, it is important to understand some of the major reasons why dogs bark endlessly.

1. Most dogs bark in order to protect their territory, they could bark ceaselessly if they feel like you are intruding their privacy.
2. Some dogs bark because they have been trained to bark therefore asking the dog not to bark will be like you are preventing them from doing their jobs and this will only lead to more barking.
3. Certain dogs bark when they are in unfamiliar situations or if they are faced with an unfamiliar problem, movement or sight. Getting control of our dog and controlling this kind of barking is very vital.
4. If you put your dog in an unfamiliar environment and you are not there it could experience some sort of anxiety and this might lead it to bark endlessly.
5. At times, by barking a dog shows other dogs that it is also where it is and at that instance the dog barks in a bid to show its identity. For those that know this kind of bark, it is very short and sharp; it shows the excitement in the dog.
6. Anxiety can get your dog to bark at its loudest over time, its anger

tends to be on a rapid increase when it is as a result of anxiety.

7. If you fail to exercise your dog, then is prepared to have a noisy dog that would not stop barking or being restless.

8. Putting dogs into tight confinements can cause to be uncomfortable and eventually lead to restlessness and discomfort in the dog.

9. Your dog is at its likeliest to bark when it is going to negative emotions like frustration, loneliness and the likes. Also, it is important to provide ways to let out energy and avoid and overflow of energy.

10. No matter how 'anti-barking' you are there are some barks that you will be pleased with. If you dog is barking in a bid to pass across crucial information to you then it will be welcome to bark at those important times. There are certain moments when a dog gets super excited because of an event or the return of a loved one or for any other reasons. Dogs can bark as a means of showing excitement.

Chapter 8

Your Dog Loves to Communicate With You

Here is some additional advice I received.
- Often times, your dog needs your attention and it is not fair if they have to resort to barking as a means of getting your attention. Encourage your dog to do certain gestures by doing it yourself in the process of teaching the dog.
- There has to be a command that you say out to ensure that your dog stops barking and stay quiet because you asked it to.
- Often times your dog will bark due to certain circumstances beyond your control (e.g. the barking of a neighbor's dogs). In situations like this, it is better to call the attention of the dog by playing with her or by doing something to get her attention.
- You are responsible for teaching your dog the "quiet" command and this command helps it to know when to keep quiet. You could give it new methods with which it can ask for food or any other thing that it needs.
- Also, it is important to recognize and cut off your dog's excesses. I used to have a dog that didn't like it when other people touched her food. I intentionally gave different people her meals to serve her at different times, with time she gets used to it.

Chapter 9
15 Easy Solutions to Use Right Now

In previous charters I have taken time to discuss why it is important to find out reason why your dog is barking. Controlling the behavior can only be done by first finding out the cause of its endless barking. What do you to handle the continuous barking of your dog? I have taken out 15 things that all pet owners should do when it comes to handling a barking dog;

1. A dog's worst nightmare is being left alone for long periods of time, as much as possible; always try to prevent your dog from being alone.

2. Avoid punishments as much as possible because not only does it cause the animal pain but also because it is not as effective as giving out rewards to the dog.

3. If you have put in your best efforts into attempting to control your dog's barking and your efforts don't seem to be yielding any meaningful results, then you should consult a professional that knows about animal behaviors.
4. Always practice basic commands with your dog until it is very familiar with it.
5. Ensure that your dog gets enough exercise in order to shed the excess energy and dogs have.
6. Be consistent in training your dog on how to bark. You should not encourage some form of barking today and then discourage it or something similar tomorrow. Help your dog to understand the standards that you have set and stay consistent with it.
7. In all that you do, remember that barking in return to a barking dog might only lead to more barking and it doesn't help you to stop it.
8. There are certain actions that encourage a barking dog and we do not even know. There are times when we awaken the curiosity of

the dog by making it seem like we have seen something weird and unusual. Dog can read human expressions and they would know when you are startles and they also tend to feel that way when you feel like that too.
9. By all means necessary, try to prevent your dog from having to bark consistently outdoors. No matter what the reason behind such barking is, it is never right to allow your dog bark in public because that could be seen as disturbance of public peace.
10. Never allow your dog to go through certain inhumane treatments in a bid to make corrections, no matter what you are trying to correct.
11. Whenever your dog is barking for a negative reason like seeking attention or barking needlessly, you should never show signs that you are encouraging such behavior example of such sign is by hugging or kissing the dog.
12. Some dog owners like using the muzzle to control the actions of their dogs. Doing this for a long time is however inhumane as it makes the dog to be totally uncomfortable for the pet.
13. Whenever your dog is barking, get its attention by doing something and then after you must have gotten its attention then you should try to make it pay attention on other productive things.
14. Unless it is expressly advised by a qualified animal specialist, you should never make use of punishments as a method of training your dog.

15. It is important for you to make your dog understand the importance of speaking and being quiet. By doing this constantly will help your dog to understand when and when not to bark.

Chapter 10

Have Confidence That You Can Train Your Dog

At this point you should understand that your dog has different kinds of barking and for different reasons, it is necessary to follow the following steps in a bid to train your dog and prevent it from barking unnecessarily. These simple and easy to follow steps include;

1. Providing more exercise for your dog; by providing more forms or variety of exercise, the gets more relaxed and will likely bark less.

2. Give it rewards; whenever you are able to get your dog to stop barking, it helps if you can offer it a reward for its silence.

3. Ignore when it barks for attention; if you constantly ignore your dog when it expects attention from you by barking, it will learn to device better methods of seeking for your attention.
4. Teach your dog to listen to orders; No one loves to have an uncontrollable pet, if you constantly give orders out to your pet and ensure that it understands these orders then your dog will definitely bark less as you would be able to command it to stop barking.
5. Give your dog duties; Dogs generally were designed to do certain duties and in the absence of these duties the dog has the tendency of getting bored and barking more often. Give your dog interactive toys to work with and watch it get creative and bark less.
6. Don't forget to teach her to speak and be quiet; a trained dog will likely understand when it has to be quite and the times when it is necessary to not be quiet. By training your dog adequately on the importance of silence, it will definitely bark less.
7. Don't encourage triggers; as a dog owner you must come to a point when you know the factors that trigger or encourage your dog to bark. It is important to discourage these factors and ensure

that the dog is kept far away from them.
8. Use training tools for ease; over time, experts on the treatment of dogs and understanding the behavior of dogs have made tools that make it easy to train dogs. Purchasing these materials will help you to get more familiar with your and it also doesn't come with as much stress as having to train your dog manually.
9. Dogs are more likely to bark when certain people visit due to the importance that such a visitor have your dog. By denying your dog access to the front door or by removing her perceived importance by asking guests not to pay attention on her. By doing this the dog is less likely to bark.

Chapter 11

Evaluating the Need for a Watch Dog

Having a watchdog has been known to help us to discover when unusual things are happening and because barking is a primary way of communication by watchdogs, then there is little that can be done about it. A baring watchdog might not totally be a bad idea but then when its barking becomes too regular then it can be a constant reason for concern.

It is in the nature of dogs to bark therefore any breed of dogs can become a watchdog as long as its barking is encouraged. The deal watchdog knows how to bark moderately and know not to harass the people around but that doesn't apply to all watchdogs. Because it is in the nature of dogs to bark then it is important to either encourage, discourage or control the level of your dog's barking. But for watchdogs, it is important that they recognize potential threats because it is a vital part of their job description.

It is important to understand the difference between a watchdog and a guard dog as one as clear as the blue skies. Watchdogs tend to be smaller and the role can be taken by almost any breed of dogs. Guard dogs on the other hand are bigger and can barely pass as mere household pets because of their large and imposing body frame. They feel the need to be protective of both people and property. In spite of these natural instincts to protect, these guard dogs can be loving gentle if trained to be social from birth or since it was a puppy.

Despite their natural protective instincts, these dogs can be gentle and loving family members, if socialized and trained early in life.

Chapter 12

Our Responsibilities to our Neighbors

In a developed society like ours, it is impossible to have a dog that disturbs everyone without having certain consequences. Local authorities may come to give your warning if your dog keeps being a nuisance (by barking at awkward times of the day) to the community where you reside. It is important to find lasting solutions to a barking dog because by doing this you are preventing heavy fines or having to move your dog away from its present location.

Civilized societies have laws that guide the behaviors of your dogs and the knowledge of these laws will help you to prevent the frustration that comes from hearing endless barking.
Different strokes for different folks, various neighbors have different methods of reacting to the problem of having a barking dog; while some might go with the direct approach and talk to the owner of such a dog, others will go on and be hostile to the dog and its owners.

What do you do when it seems like you have a problematic dog that just seems to have the tendency of causing you so much troubles with law enforcement and your neighbors? Make a move before your neighbors begin to complain about it, you can train your dog to do the right things and you won't have to answer queries from your neighbors.

A dog that barks appropriately will ultimately save you from trouble from both neighbor's complaints and also helps you see danger before it materializes and becomes too late to respond properly. Having a dog that barks at the right time can save you from danger and call attention to you when you need it. For examples, if you become unconscious your dog can save you by barking to get the attention of people around you.

Chapter 13

Puppies are Often Too Cute to Resist

Not everyone would like to have a grown dog because of the obvious troubles that come with owning one. When it comes to owning a puppy on the other hand, you can barely see people that are not in love with these tiny, cute and cuddly pets. As cute as puppies are, they certainly learn to bark after a while and often times become too noisy when they try to get your attention for whatever reason by barking. I will give you this piece of first-hand information as gotten from the Veterinary services department, Dr. Foster and Smith, incorporation.

"Teaching your puppy appropriate behavior from the beginning is easier than changing behavior that has become a bad habit. Some behavior we may think of as cute in a puppy will not be cute in an adult dog. So, think ahead to avoid potential problems…

The first few nights after bringing your puppy home will be the hardest. You may want to put his crate in your bedroom. The puppy will be more secure with you near. Security builds trust. Trust will decrease the possibility of separation anxiety in the future. Just remember not to give any attention to the puppy if he is whining – that will only reward his undesirable behavior.

By starting to train your puppy in obedience and relaxation at an early age, you can greatly reduce the probability your puppy will grow into a problem barker. Nip problems in the bud and always look at why the puppy is barking. Is it fear, anxiety, attention-seeking? Use the appropriate measures to treat the underlying problem.

Remember that if for some reason you want your dog to bark on command, or in a certain situation, you must also be able to teach her to stop on command. Teach "Enough" at an early age. This was described under "Alert/warning Barkers".

Introduce the young puppy to situations that may cause anxiety later on. Get your puppy used to walking on the sidewalk along a busy street.

Expose your puppy to sounds like vacuum cleaners, hair dryers, and other noises. Take things slow so your puppy does not become anxious while being exposed to these new things. Reward the puppy when he is quiet and relaxed.

Puppy classes are a great place for your puppy to meet new people and other dogs. He can learn to obey you even when there are numerous distractions. You also have a trainer present who can help you with any potential problems.

In short, it will be a lot more fun for everybody if your puppy learns to communicate through a wag of the tail and looking to you for guidance rather than through excessive and relentless barking."

Chapter 14

Pet Owners Have Responsibilities

The older a dog gets, the more difficult it is to train the dogs about certain things therefore it is important to begin training your dog at a very early stage of its life in order to ensure that it follows your teaching. Having a nuisance dog that doesn't know when to stop barking could be very frustrating; not only to the neighbors but also to the pet owner. The pertinent problem now has to be how to ensure that you exercise enough patience to be able to adequately and properly training the dog. The decision to become a dog owner is a full-time decision that has to be done with a lot of dedication and zeal to ensure maximal results. Often times I compare raising a dog to raising a child because in both cases you are trying to show both beings the difference between right and wrong. In raising a dog, you have to constantly show the difference between right and right and endeavor to stay consistent in how you decide to train your dog,

At times it gets so frustrating for me as a dog owner, so frustrating that at times I feel like hitting her out of anger. Since I have learnt that this method doesn't help and instead it causes the dog to become more scared and bark out of fear. Also, the use of shock collards and other forms of punishment will only cause the pet to me more traumatized, when training your dog, it is important to understand the negative effects of raising your voice at your pet and avoid it altogether. Also, the way you react to your dogs barking will go a long way in telling it whether you are encouraging or discouraging the gesture. Dogs get very jealous and emotional therefore it is important to give it the attention that it requires.

In raising a dog, you need to have and exercise a certain level of discipline and this does not even involve showing physical violence. Understanding that the dog is a member of the family and treating it that way will go a long way in regulating the barking and other behaviors of the pet. By properly regulating the behavior of your pet then you are able to make your relationship with the canine more rewarding.

Chapter 15
From Other Dog Experts

Once again, I will share some knowledge as gotten from another dog expert and lover who gave practical methods and information when it comes to training your dogs.

He said; *"Training a dog can be done relatively easily, despite what some people believe. You simply have to keep a few training tips in mind. You must teach the dog that you are in charge, and not her. You must also use a tone that exudes superiority and confidence. Lastly, you absolutely must be consistent in your training methods. Learn to master these three tips and your dog will learn whatever you want to teach her.*

You're in charge. Even when you see your dog's adorable face, you must keep in mind that you are the one giving commands and your dog must obey your commands. If you're too soft with your dog and let her be in charge, your rug, shoes and many other belongings will likely suffer. That's not mentioning the other people who will be affected by your dog's lack of good manners. Set boundaries and let your dog know what is and isn't appropriate. Use appropriate tone of voice and gestures like pointing.

Be strict. You know the expression "give an inch and take a mile"? That's exactly what will happen to your dog if you are not consistently strict. Dogs can sense if you are being strict by your tone of voice. Be strict and use appropriate tone when you order her to stay in the yard. If you want to go out for a walk, you don't have to use the same tone. Be enthusiastic instead. If your dog starts running away, be strict again and he'll understand who's in charge.

Be consistent. You must maintain a certain consistency in intonations, gestures and words when dealing with your dog. Otherwise, the dog may get confused. Always use the same commands and always act the same way when he does something that is unacceptable. By being consistent, your dog will become better trained, which will improve your confidence in your training skills. The more confident you are, the better trained your dog will be! You can also establish consistency in your actions by always using the same door to take the dog out or by always using the same nighttime routine.

By being in charge, strict and consistent, you can better train your dog and better predict his behavior. Don't forget to show your love and affection for your dog as well! Treat your training sessions as games and reward her for his good actions."

Chapter 16

Stop and Listen to Your Dog

Often times, we tend to attribute barking to only the dogs while forgetting that we could be the cause, how can we cause our pets to bark more? It is more about not paying enough attention to the needs of the dog both physically and emotionally. I will again leave you the advice of a professional, this time Dr. Mayra Alfonso;

"*Fundamentally, dog behavior training is basically about communicating with the pet. From a human perspective, the trainer is the one who communicates to the puppy which conducts are desirable and which ones are not positive, as well as circumstantial conducts and when to do what. From the dog's perspective, the trainer must in addition understand what things inspire the puppy to help reach unsurpassed results.*
Applying extremely consistent hand signals as well as verbal commands would enable your dog to comprehend them more quickly. It is additionally important to note that the prize of the dog is not similar as the reward marker. The reward marker is a dog hand signal that allows the pup to understand that he has earned a prize.
A prize can be a treat, a dog toy or anything else that a pet will find pleasing. If you neglect to prize the dog after doing the reward hand signal, then the significance of the reward gets smaller, thus making the dog training harder. Using classical conditioning you can also teach your furry friend the punishment marker in conjunction with the punishment itself. But recall that dogs cannot generalize commands very freely. A hand signal which might be effective in the house might cause confusion for them the minute you do it out of the house. So, the dog command would need to be instructed further in every unfamiliar occasion.
As for punishment the trainer has to take into consideration what's applicable to the pet's identity, experience, age as well as their mental and physical conditions. A firm "no" works on many pups but there are those that demonstrate signs of apprehension or terror towards tough verbal corrections. Negative reinforcement should also only be applied if the

unacceptable puppy behavior is something that can be rapidly corrected, and the punishment should never entail physical punishment. Dog behavior training should be fun for you

Chapter 17
What To Do When it Gets Legal

As I said earlier, in developed where dogs are seen as a part of the family, there are rules against owners of problematic pets. The duty of ensuring that these dogs do not go against the laws rests mainly on the pet owner who ha to ensure that the dog does not cause him to pay heavily in terms of fines.

It is important to know what the law says about barking both in your locality and in your larger society. Knowing what these laws are will help you in training your pet to ensure that their behavior is in line with the provisions of the law. In case of lawsuit for or against you because of the barking of a dog, there are certain issues that are important and must be addressed. They include;

1. Properly considering if the barking of the dog will affect the average person in the position of the person complaining.

2. It is also pivotal to point out how the barking interferes with the enjoyable use of the property by the person who owns it.

3. Before attention can be given to any complaint concerning a barking dog, the person complaining must have proof that clearly explain the damages caused as a result of the barking canine.

4. If the lawsuit doesn't work out then both parties are urged to try mediation in order to arrive at a conclusive decision that will be in the best interest of both parties that are involved in the lawsuit. All these can be avoided if we decide to do our part in ensuring the dog does not become a nuisance.

Made in the USA
Middletown, DE
18 December 2022